DIPLODOCUS

By Thomas George

Gareth Stevens
PUBLISHING

leveled
reader

Please visit our website, www.garethstevens.com. For a free color catalog of all our high-quality books, call toll free 1-800-542-2595 or fax 1-877-542-2596.

Library of Congress Cataloging-in-Publication Data

George, Thomas.
Diplodocus / by Thomas George.
p. cm. — (A look at dinosaurs)
Includes index.
ISBN 978-1-4824-1822-4 (pbk.)
ISBN 978-1-4824-1821-7 (6-pack)
ISBN 978-1-4824-1823-1 (library binding)
1. Diplodocus — Juvenile literature. I. Title.
QE862.S3 G46 2015
567.913—d23

Published in 2015 by
Gareth Stevens Publishing
111 East 14th Street, Suite 349
New York, NY 10003

Designer: Nicholas Domiano
Editor: Ryan Nagelhout

Illustrations by Jeffrey Mangiat
Science Consultant: Darla Zelenitsky, Ph.D.,
Assistant Professor of Dinosaur Paleontology at the University of Calgary, Canada

Printed in the United States of America

CPSIA compliance information: Batch #CW15GS: For further information contact Gareth Stevens, New York, New York at 1-800-542-2595.

Contents

Boldface words appear in the glossary.

Meet *Diplodocus*

What was the *Diplodocus* (duh-PLAH-duh-kuhs)? It was a dinosaur in the sauropod family. Sauropods were plant-eating dinosaurs with a long neck, long tail, and four legs. They were the largest land animals that ever lived. The *Diplodocus* was longer than two city buses!

5

Finding Fossils

Many *Diplodocus* **fossils** have been found in North America. Scientists think they lived in the areas that are now Wyoming, Utah, Colorado, and New Mexico. We can learn a lot about the *Diplodocus* by studying its fossils.

UNITED STATES

Wyoming

Utah

Colorado

New Mexico

north

west ← → east

south

Key

= *Diplodocus* lived here

7

"Double Beam"

Diplodocus fossils show that this dinosaur had a long neck and an even longer tail. The long tail helped the *Diplodocus* balance. The name *Diplodocus* means "double beam." This comes from the special shape of the bones in its tail.

neck

tail

9

Fighting Predators, *Diplodocus*-Style!

The *Diplodocus* was very tall and very heavy. Because it was so big, the *Diplodocus* moved slowly. How did it fight off faster **predators**? It used its tail. Scientists think the *Diplodocus* could **whip** its tail at 800 miles (1,287 km) per hour!

A Giant Plant Eater

It took a lot of food to feed the giant *Diplodocus*. It ate thousands of pounds of food a day. The *Diplodocus* was a plant eater, or **herbivore**. Herbivores only eat plants. The *Diplodocus* probably ate pine trees and other leafy plants.

Finding Food
the *Diplodocus* Way

The *Diplodocus* was too big to walk through forests. But its body's special shape helped it get food in a different way. The *Diplodocus*'s long neck reached the tops of trees. Its short legs helped it reach plants near the ground.

Special Teeth

An all-plant diet **requires** special teeth. Luckily, the *Diplodocus*'s teeth were pretty special. Its 40 large teeth were shaped like pegs. They pointed slightly forward. This made the *Diplodocus*'s teeth perfect for taking the leaves off branches.

Nest Eggs

Diplodocus eggs were like other sauropods' eggs. Most were the size of a grapefruit, but some eggs reached the size of a football. Although the eggs were big, the shells weren't too thick. Baby *Diplodocuses* could still break out of them.

A Herd of *Diplodocuses*

It would be amazing to see just one giant *Diplodocus*, but imagine seeing many of them grouped together. This probably happened often, since they traveled in **herds**. This was especially important for young *Diplodocuses*. Traveling in herds kept them safe.

Glossary

fossil: the hardened marks or remains of plants and animals that formed over thousands or millions of years

herbivore: an animal that eats only plants

herd: a group of animals that live, eat, and travel together

predator: an animal that hunts other animals for food

require: to have a need for

whip: to move fast or suddenly

For More Information

Books

Dixon, Dougal. *Everything You Need to Know About Dinosaurs*. New York, NY: Kingfisher, 2012.

Rockwood, Leigh. *Diplodocus*. New York, NY: PowerKids Press, 2012.

Websites

The Dino Directory: Diplodocus
nhm.ac.uk/nature-online/life/dinosaurs-other-extinct-creatures/dino-directory/diplodocus.html#
The website for the London Natural History Museum provides interesting information about the *Diplodocus*.

Walking with Dinosaurs: Diplodocus
walkingwithdinosaurs.com/dinosaurs/detail/diplodocus/
The British Broadcasting Company's website for the movie *Walking with Dinosaurs* teaches cool facts about the *Diplodocus* and other dinosaurs.

Index